PASS YOUR
GCSE MATHS
Measures

Dear Student,

Thank you for buying this book. It will help you with your GCSE Maths by showing you how to gain extra marks. Just one of those marks could move you up a grade. Remember that there is only one mark difference between a Grade D and a Grade C.

Most of the double page spreads in the book consist of three sections: 'What You Need to Know', 'Revision Facts' and 'Questions'.

Read 'What You Need to Know' carefully, making sure that it makes sense to you. You may find it helpful to work with someone else so that you can check that each other understands.

Use the 'Revision Facts' as a reminder — you may like to copy these into an exercise book to create a revision guide to use nearer your exam.

Try all the 'Questions', even those that are easy but especially those that appear to be difficult. There is an answer section in the centre that you can pull out so that you can check your work. If you find that you have made a mistake, don't worry but just try to see where you went wrong. You can learn a lot from mistakes.

To answer some of the questions you may need a ruler, a pair of compasses, a protractor or a calculator.

Good luck,

Andrew Brodie

WHAT YOU NEED TO KNOW

The perimeter of a shape is the distance all the way around it. (Think of a perimeter fence.)

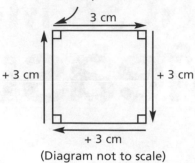

Always choose a start and finish point.

3 cm

+ 3 cm   + 3 cm

+ 3 cm

(Diagram not to scale)

You can see that the perimeter of the square is 12 cm.

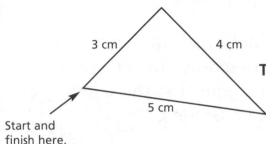

3 cm   4 cm

5 cm

Start and finish here.

The perimeter of this triangle = 3 + 4 + 5 = 12 cm.

The perimeter of a circle is called the circumference.
The radius (r) is the distance from the centre to the edge.
The circumference of a circle is found using this formula: $C = 2 \pi r$

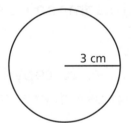

3 cm

The circumference of this circle is:

$C = 2 \pi r$
$= 2 \times 3.142 \times 3$
$= 18.852$

(3.142 is an approximate value for π.)

You could have found the answer by using the calculator, pressing these keys:

 2 x π x 3 =

(You may find that on your calculator you need to press the shift key **SHIFT** and then the EXP key **EXP** to get π.)

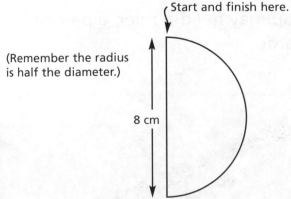

Start and finish here.

(Remember the radius is half the diameter.)

8 cm

If this was a whole circle the circumference would be

$$2 \pi r = 2 \times \pi \times 4 = 25.136$$

but it's only half a circle (a semi-circle) so divide 25.136 by 2:

$$25.136 \div 2 = 12.568 \text{ cm}$$

... but this only gives the curved part, so add on the 8 cm.

The total perimeter is 20.568 cm.

REVISION FACTS

✓ The perimeter of a shape is the distance all the way round it.

✓ The circumference of a circle = 2 π r (this is the same as π d).

✓ Make sure you use the same units, i.e. measure everything in cm <u>or</u> m <u>or</u> mm but don't mix them up.

QUESTIONS

Find the perimeters of these shapes. Note that they are not drawn to scale. (The examiners will often set questions with diagrams not drawn to scale.) Show your workings and write your answer clearly on the dotted line. You will need to write your answers to an appropriate degree of accuracy. This means that you will have to decide whether to round your answers to whole numbers or to one decimal place or two decimal places.

1

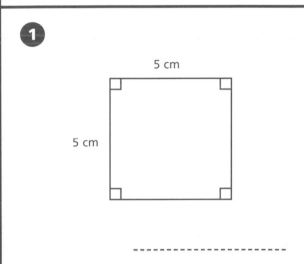

5 cm

5 cm

2

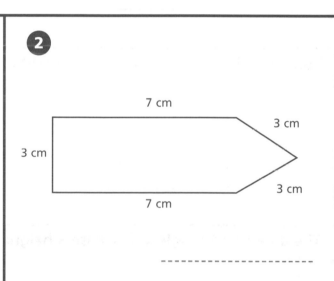

7 cm

3 cm

3 cm

3 cm

3 cm

7 cm

3

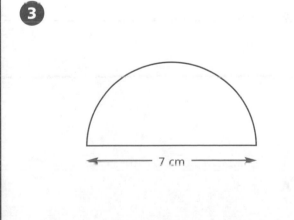

← 7 cm →

4

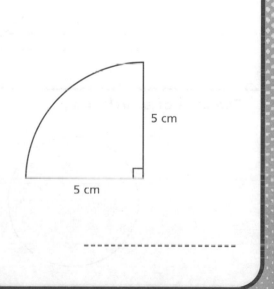

5 cm

5 cm

WHAT YOU NEED TO KNOW

The area of a shape is the amount of space it covers. You can see that this square covers 9 square centimetres.

The area of a square = length of side x length of side.

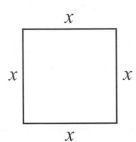

This square has sides of length x.

Area = x x x

A = x^2

The area of a rectangle = length x width.

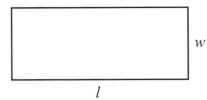

A = lw (Remember, when letters are pushed together they are multiplying, ie. $lw = l$ x w.)

The area of a triangle = $\frac{1}{2}$ x base x height.

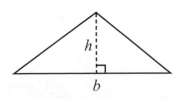

A = $\frac{1}{2}bh$ (or 0.5 x b x h)

The area of a circle = πr^2

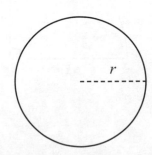

A = πr^2

REVISION FACT

$A = x^2$ | $A = lw$ | $A = \frac{1}{2} bh$ | $A = \pi r^2$

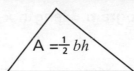

Examples:

1.

4.1 cm
4.1 cm

Find the area of this square.

$$A = 4.1^2$$

On the calculator you could press:

or

Both will give you the same answer.
The answer is 16.81 cm²

2.

2.7 cm

Find the area of this circle.

$$A = \pi r^2$$
$$= \pi \times 2.7^2$$

On the calculator you could press:

(Note on some calculators you need to press **SHIFT** **EXP** to get π)

or

Both will give you the same answer.
The answer is 22.9 cm²

QUESTIONS

Find the area of each of these shapes. Show your workings, and answer on the dotted line.

1

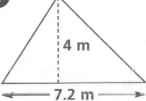
4 m
7.2 m

2

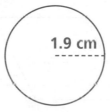
1.9 cm

3

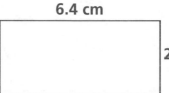
6.4 cm
2.3 cm

- - - - - - - - - - - - - - -   - - - - - - - - - - - - - - -   - - - - - - - - - - - - - - -

WHAT YOU NEED TO KNOW

The area of a parallelogram = length x height

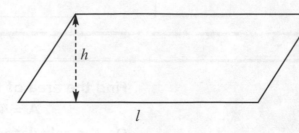

A = *lh*

(The opposite sides of a parallelogram are equal, just like a rectangle, but the corners are not 90°.)

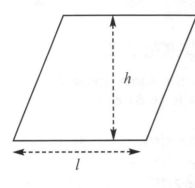

The area of a rhombus = length x height

A = *lh*

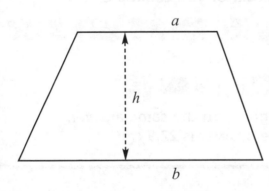

The area of a trapezium = $\frac{1}{2}$ x (a + b) x height

A = $\frac{1}{2}(a + b)h$

REVISION FACT

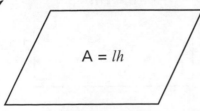

A = *lh*

parallelogram

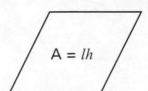

A = *lh*

rhombus

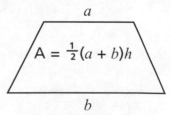

A = $\frac{1}{2}(a + b)h$

trapezium

Examples:

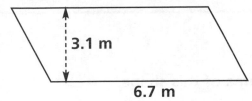

Find the area of this parallelogram.

$$A = lh$$
$$= 6.7 \times 3.1$$
$$= 20.77 \text{ m}^2$$

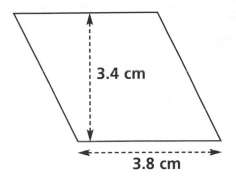

Find the area of this rhombus.

$$A = lh$$
$$= 3.8 \times 3.4$$
$$= 12.92 \text{ cm}^2$$

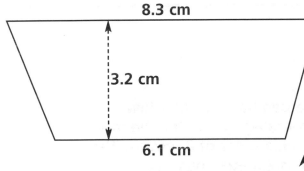

Find the area of this trapezium.

$$A = \tfrac{1}{2}(a + b)\,h$$
$$= \tfrac{1}{2}(8.3 + 6.1) \times 3.2$$
$$= 23.04 \text{ cm}^2$$

These are the calculator keys you must press:

| 0 | · | 5 | x | (| 8 | · | 3 | + | 6 | · | 1 |) | x | 3 | · | 2 | = |

The brackets are crucial.

QUESTIONS

Find the areas of these shapes. Show your workings, and answer on the dotted line.

1

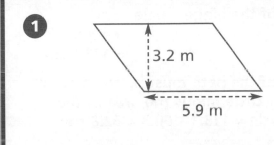

....

2

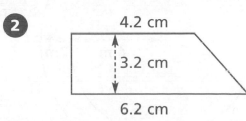

....

WHAT YOU NEED TO KNOW

These are examples of more complicated questions.

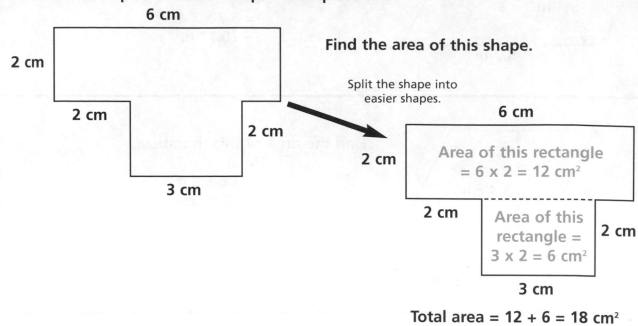

Find the area of this shape.

Split the shape into easier shapes.

Area of this rectangle = 6 x 2 = 12 cm²

Area of this rectangle = 3 x 2 = 6 cm²

Total area = 12 + 6 = 18 cm²

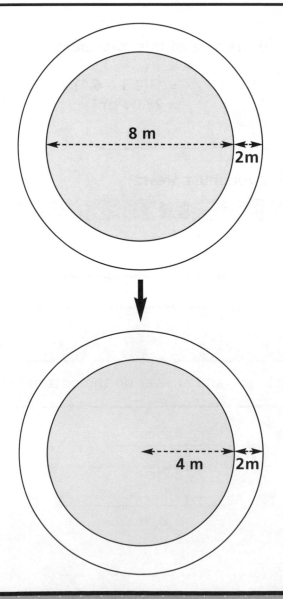

A garden has a circular lawn surrounded by a path. The lawn has a diameter of 8 metres. The path is 2 metres wide.
What is the area of the path?

The area we are interested in is the ring around the edge.

The radius of the smaller circle = 4 m. (The radius is half the diameter)
The area of the smaller circle = πr^2
$= \pi \times 4^2$
$= 50.3$ cm²

The area of the bigger circle $= \pi r^2$
$= \pi \times 6^2$
$= 113.1$ cm²

The area of the path must be the area of the bigger circle minus the area of the smaller circle = 113.1 − 50.3 = 62.8 cm²

QUESTIONS

Find the areas of these shapes. Show your workings.

1

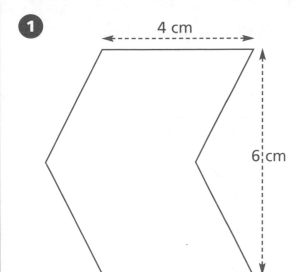

4 cm

6 cm

2

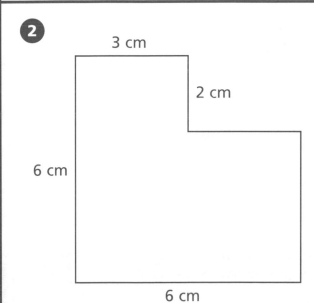

3 cm

2 cm

6 cm

6 cm

3

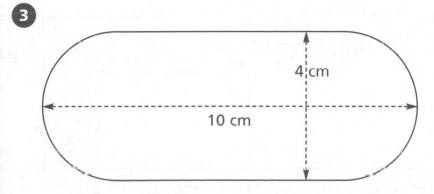

4 cm

10 cm

Clue: make this shape into a rectangle and two semi-circles.

WHAT YOU NEED TO KNOW

The volume of a prism =

Area of cross-section x length.

The easiest cross-section to use is the end of the shape.

Here is a cuboid.
A cuboid is a type of prism.

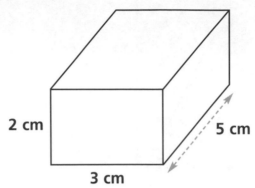

2 cm

5 cm

3 cm

The end of this cuboid is a rectangle.
The area of the rectangle = 2 x 3 = 6 cm²

The length of the cuboid is 5 cm.

… so the volume = Area of end x length

= 6 x 5

= 30 cm³

Notice that the answer is given in cubic centimetres.
You could gain an extra mark by remembering to write cm³.

The easiest volume to find is the volume of a cube.
A cube has equal sized edges.

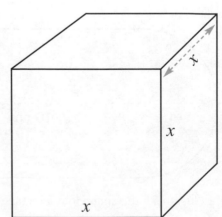

x

x

x

The volume is the area of the end x length.
In the diagram this would be x **x** x **x** x

This is the area
of the end.

This is the
length.

REVISION FACT

✓ Volume = Area of end x length.

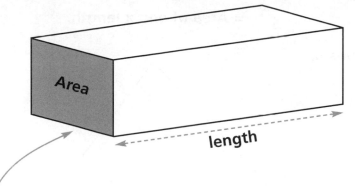

Area

length

Look how the picture is drawn.
This end _is_ a rectangle although because of
the way it's drawn you can't see right angles.

QUESTIONS

Find the volumes of these cuboids. Show your workings.

1

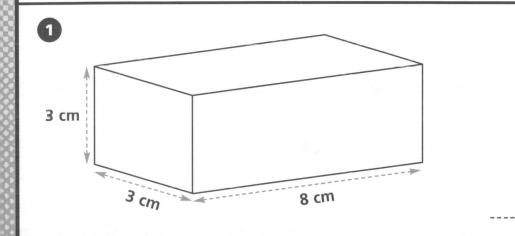

3 cm

3 cm   8 cm

2

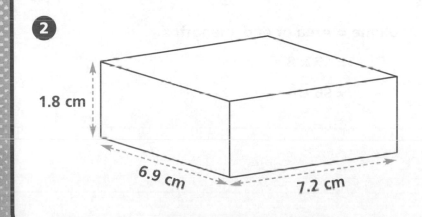

1.8 cm

6.9 cm   7.2 cm

WHAT YOU NEED TO KNOW

Remember: the volume of a prism

= Area of end x length.

Look at this triangular prism:

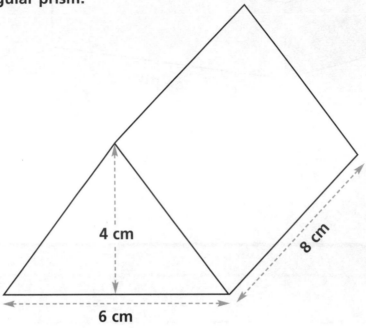

Step 1: Find the area of the end.

$$\text{Area of triangle} = \tfrac{1}{2} \times \text{base} \times \text{height}$$

$$= \tfrac{1}{2} \times 6 \times 4$$

$$= 3 \times 4$$

$$= 12 \text{ cm}^2$$

square centimetres for area

Step 2: Find the volume.

$$\text{Volume} = \text{Area of end} \times \text{length}$$

$$= 12 \times 8$$

$$= 96 \text{ cm}^3$$

cubic centimetres for volume

QUESTIONS

Find the volumes of these triangular prisms. Show your workings.

1

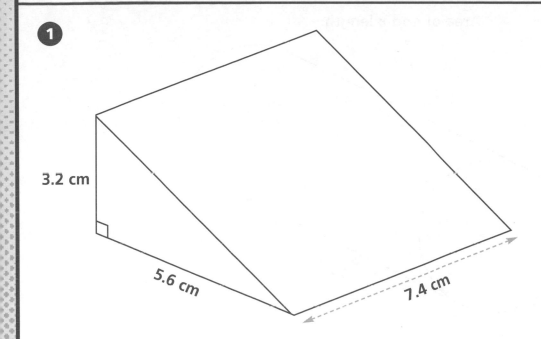

3.2 cm

5.6 cm

7.4 cm

2

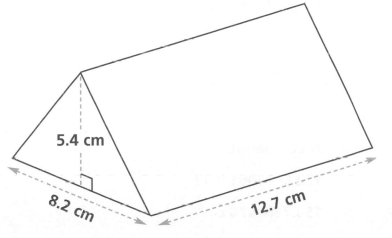

5.4 cm

8.2 cm

12.7 cm

WHAT YOU NEED TO KNOW

Volume of a cylinder =

Area of end x length.

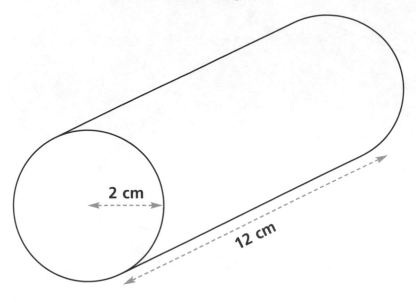

2 cm

12 cm

Step 1: Find the area of the end.

Area of a circle = π r²

$$= π \times 2^2$$

$$= π \times 4$$

$$= 12.56637061 \text{ cm}^2$$

That's what the calculator shows.
Leave it on the calculator screen.

Step 2: Find the volume.

Volume = Area x length

$$= 12.56637061 \times 12$$

$$= 150.7964474 \text{ cm}^3$$

That's what the calculator shows.

$$= 151 \text{ cm}^3$$

To the nearest cubic centimetre.

p3.	1. 20 cm 2. 23 cm

3. $2\pi r = 2 \times \pi \times 3.5$. The calculator shows 21.99114858. But we need <u>half</u> the circle so divide this by 2 to get 10.99557429. Round this to 11 because 10.99557429 is very nearly 11. We also need to add on the straight line: 11 + 7 = <u>18 cm</u>.

4. $2\pi r = 2 \times \pi \times 5$. The calculator shows 31.41592654. Don't round this yet. We want a quarter of the circle so just divide by 4. This gives 7.853981634. Now round this to 1 decimal place: 7.9. We also need to add on both straight lines: 5 + 5 + 7.9 = 17.9 cm.

---

p5.

1. Area $= \frac{1}{2}\, bh$

$= \frac{1}{2} \times 7.2 \times 4$

$= 14.4$ cm^2

Don't forget the little ^{2} for area.

2. Area $= \pi r^2$

$= \pi \times 1.9^2$

$= 11.34$ cm^2

3. Area $= lw$

$= 6.4 \times 2.3$

$= 14.72$ cm^2

---

p7.

1. Area $= lh$

$= 5.9 \times 3.2$

$= 18.88$ cm^2

2. Area $= \frac{1}{2}(a + b)h$

$= \frac{1}{2}(4.2 + 6.2) \times 3.2$

$= \frac{1}{2} \times 10.4 \times 3.2$

$= 0.5 \times 10.4 \times 3.2$

$= 16.64$ cm^2

---

p9.

1. This shape is made of two parallelograms.

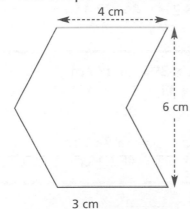

4 cm

6 cm

The height of each parallelogram is 3 cm.

Area of each parallelogram $= 4 \times 3$
$= 12$ cm^2

So total area = 24 cm^2.

2.

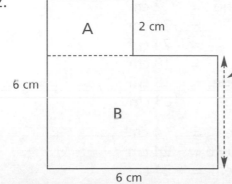

3 cm

A

2 cm

6 cm

B

6 cm

This side must be 4 cm because 6 cm − 2 cm = 4 cm.

Area of rectangle A $= 3 \times 2 = 6$ cm^2

Area of rectangle B $= 6 \times 4 = 24$ cm^2

Total Area $= 30$ cm^2.

p9.   3.

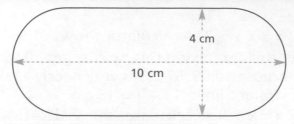

4 cm

10 cm

The diameter of the
semi-circle   = 4 cm.
So the radius = 2 cm.

The diameter of the
semi-circle = 4 cm. So the radius = 2 cm.
There is a semi-circle each side of the rectangle so the length
of the rectangle is 10 cm minus 2 cm for each semi-circle

$$= 10 - 4$$
$$= 6 \text{ cm}$$

Area of rectangle = 6 x 4 = 24 cm²
Two semi-circles = 1 whole circle
Area of circle $= \pi r^2$
                  $= \pi \times 2^2$
                  $= \pi \times 4$
                  = 12.57 cm²
Total area   = 36.57 cm²

---

p11.   1.   Area of end = 3 x 3 =   9 cm²
                Volume   = 9 x 8 = 72 cm³

         2.   Area of end = 1.8 x 6.9   = 12.42 cm²
              Volume   = 12.42 x 7.2 = 89.4 cm³ to 1 decimal place

---

p13.   1.   Area of end = 0.5 x 5.6 x 3.2 = 8.96 cm²
                Volume   = 8.96 x 7.4   = 66.3 cm³ to 1 decimal place

         2.   Area of end = 0.5 x 8.2 x 5.4 = 22.14 cm²
              Volume   = 22.14 x 12.7   = 281.2 cm³ to 1 decimal place

---

p19.   1.   Area of end = πr^2 = $\pi \times 3^2$ = 28.27 cm²
                Volume   = 28.27 x 11 = 311 cm³ to the nearest whole number
                (We can write this to the nearest whole number as this is accurate enough.)

         2.   Area of end = $\pi \times 4.2^2$ = 55.42 cm²
              Volume   = 55.42 x 8.7 = 482.1 cm³ to 1 decimal place

---

p21.   1.   Area of one end   =   12 cm²
                Area of other end =   12 cm²
                Area of top   =   24 cm²
                Area of base   =   24 cm²
                Area of side   =   18 cm²
                Area of other side =   18 cm²
                Total surface area = 108 cm²

                Area of one side   =   4 cm²
                Multiply 4 cm² by 6 =   24 cm²
                Total surface area =   24 cm²

p23.	1. Area of one triangular end = 0.5 x 6 x 4 = 12 cm²
	Area of other triangular end = 12 cm²
	Area of the base = 42 cm²
	Area of one side = 35 cm²
	Area of other side = 35 cm²
	Total surface area = 136 cm²
	
	2. C = 2πr = 2 x π x 3
	The calculator will show the answer 18.84955592. Don't round your answer yet.
	Keep this on the screen and multiply by 8 to find the area of the curved side. This gives the answer 150.7964474.
	So area of side = 150.8 to 1 decimal place.
	Area of circular end = πr²
	                                                = 28.27433388
	                                                = 28.3 to 1 decimal place.
	Area of other circular end = 28.3 to 1 decimal place.
	Total surface area = 207.4 cm²

p24.	1. a) 135° b) 225°
p26.	The bearing of ship Y from ship X is 037° ⟵ 3 digits remember.
p27.	1. 300° 2. a) 250° b) 070°
p29.	1. & 2. 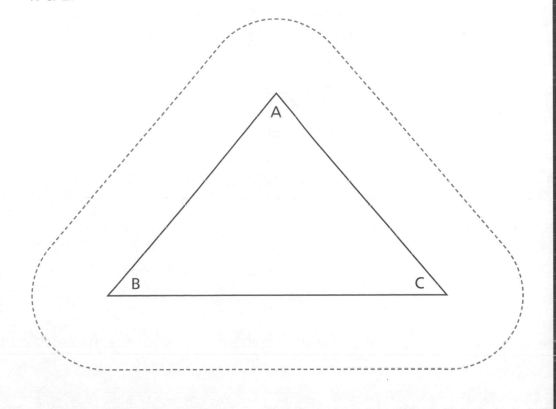

p31.   1.

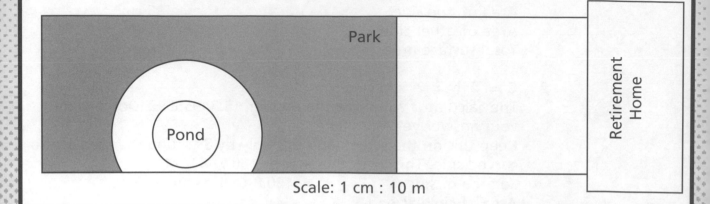

Scale: 1 cm : 10 m

p32.

1   Speed = $\frac{\text{distance}}{\text{time}}$ = $\frac{15}{0.5}$ = 30 mph

2.   Speed = $\frac{\text{distance}}{\text{time}}$ = $\frac{400}{93}$ = 4.3 m/s

This is sometimes written like this ms⁻¹ which means $\frac{m}{s}$.

3.   Speed = $\frac{\text{distance}}{\text{time}}$ = $\frac{45}{2}$ = 22.5 km/h

4. $3\frac{1}{2}$ minutes = 3.5 x 60 = 210 seconds
     Speed   = $\frac{200}{210}$ = 0.95 ms⁻¹

5.   Time = $\frac{\text{distance}}{\text{speed}}$ = 2 hours

6.   Distance = Speed x Time
                = 500 x 2.25
                = 1125 km.

because 2 hours 15 minutes is $2\frac{1}{4}$ hours.

QUESTIONS

Find the volumes of these cylinders. Show your workings.

1

(Clue: radius = $\frac{1}{2}$ of diameter.)

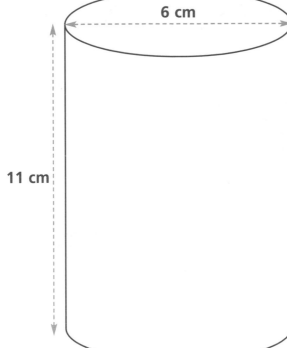

6 cm

11 cm

- -

2

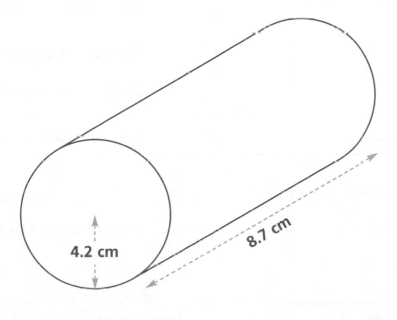

4.2 cm

8.7 cm

- -

WHAT YOU NEED TO KNOW

Sometimes you may be asked to find the surface area of a cuboid, a cylinder or a triangular prism.

Look at this cuboid:

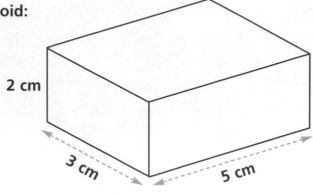

Here is the net of the cuboid.

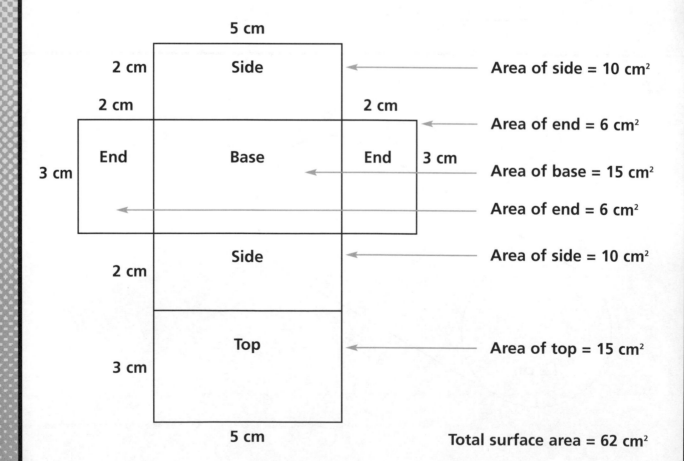

Area of side = 10 cm^2

Area of end = 6 cm^2

Area of base = 15 cm^2

Area of end = 6 cm^2

Area of side = 10 cm^2

Area of top = 15 cm^2

Total surface area = 62 cm^2

REVISION FACT

✓ Surface area of solid shape =

Area of all faces added together.

QUESTIONS

1 Find the surface area of this cuboid.

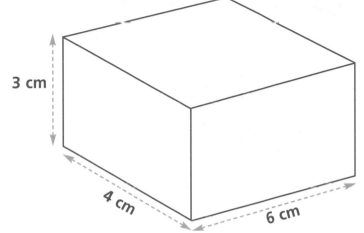

(Clue: use this system to find the area of each face.)

Area of one end	= 3 x 4 = 12cm²
Area of other end	=
Area of top	=
Area of base	=
Area of side	=
Area of other side	=
Total surface area	=

2 Find the surface area of this cube. Show your workings.

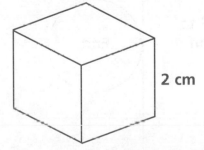

2 cm

(Clue: a cube has six equal faces, so just find the
area of one of them and multiply by six.)

WHAT YOU NEED TO KNOW

Look at the net of a triangular prism:

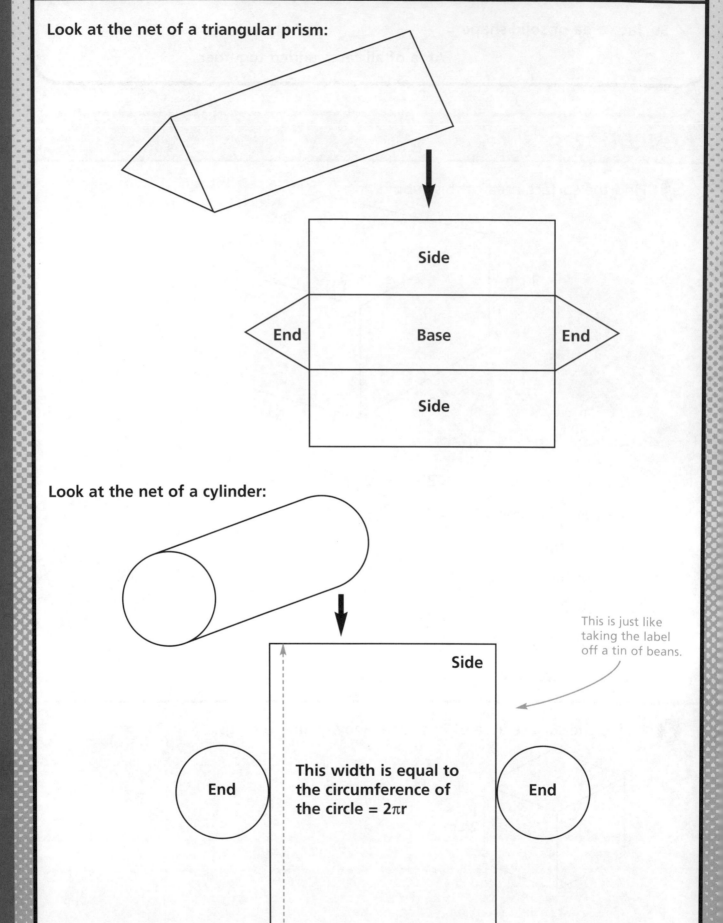

Look at the net of a cylinder:

This is just like taking the label off a tin of beans.

This width is equal to the circumference of the circle = 2πr

QUESTIONS

Find the surface areas of these solid shapes. Show your workings.

1

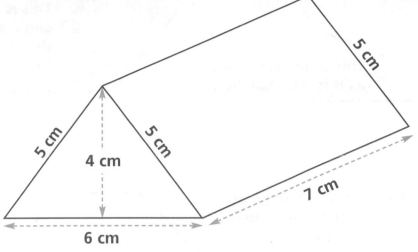

Area of one triangular end   =

Area of other triangular end   =

Area of base   =

Area of one side   =

Area of other side   =

Total surface area   =

2

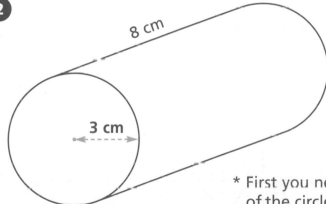

* First you need to find the circumference
   of the circle.

$$C = 2\pi r =$$

Now find the areas:

Area of side   =

Area of one circular end   =

Area of other circular end   =

Total surface area   =

WHAT YOU NEED TO KNOW

This is an acute angle as it is less than 90°.

This is an obtuse angle as it is more than 90° but less than 180°.

This is a reflex angle as it is more than 180° but less than 360°.

For more work on angles: see our book
Pass Your GCSE Maths: Angles and Triangles.

QUESTION

1a Use a protractor to measure the size of the obtuse angle. _____

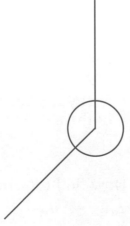

1b Calculate the size of the reflex angle.
(Remember, angles around a point add up to 360°.) _____

WHAT YOU NEED TO KNOW

Many exams will have questions about bearings.
Follow the steps in this example:

Find the bearing of the ship at point B from the lighthouse at point A.

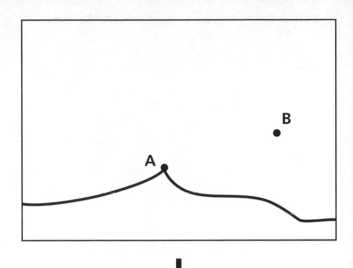

Step 1: Draw a line pointing north from point A.

Step 2: Draw a line to point B from point A.

Step 3: Measure the angle made by the two lines that you have drawn.

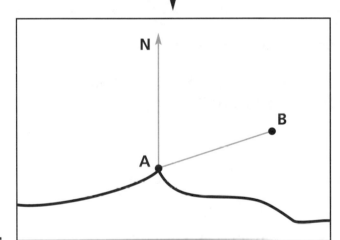

In this example, the angle measures 72°.

The bearing of the ship from the lighthouse is 072°.

Don't forget the zero as bearings must always have three digits.

REVISION FACTS

✓ Bearings always have three digits.

✓ Always consider where the question is asking you to work <u>from</u> - draw a north line there.

✓ Measure <u>clockwise</u> from the north line.

QUESTION

Find the bearing of ship Y from ship X.

• Y

X •

The bearing of ship Y from ship X is   ------------------------

WHAT YOU NEED TO KNOW

Look at this example.

Find the bearing of the lighthouse A from the ship at B.

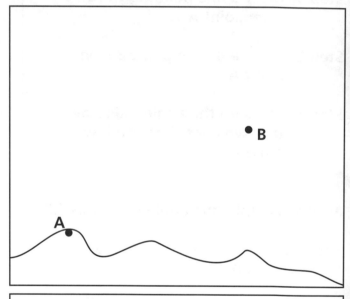

Step 1: Draw a line pointing north from the ship B.

Step 2: Draw a line to A from B.

Step 3: What we really need is the reflex angle at B but it's easier to measure the obtuse angle first.

(In this example, the obtuse angle is 120°)

Step 4: Subtract that obtuse angle from 360° to find the clockwise angle from the north line. 360 – 240 = 120

The bearing is 240°

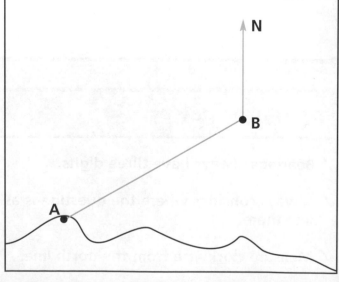

REVISION FACT

✓ **Remember that you need the clockwise angle from the north line.**

QUESTIONS

1 Find the bearing of the point P from the point Q.

• P

(Remember to draw the north line at Q. Draw a line from Q to P. Measure the acute angle between the lines you have drawn. Subtract that angle from 360° to find the clockwise angle.)

Q •

2a Find the bearing of the point V from the point W.

• W

• V

2b Find the bearing of the point W from the point V.

WHAT YOU NEED TO KNOW

The word loci is the plural of the word locus.

The locus of a point is the path that it takes when it obeys certain rules.

Rule: the point is always an equal distance from X and Y.

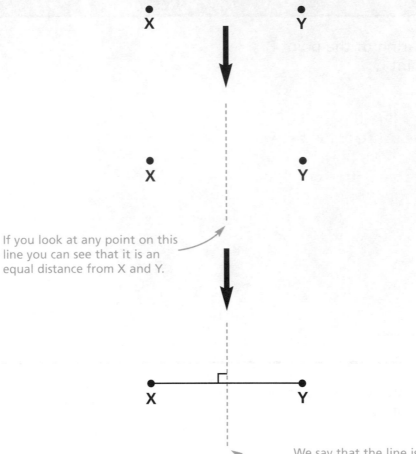

If you look at any point on this line you can see that it is an equal distance from X and Y.

We say that the line is the perpendicular bisector of line XY.

(Perpendicular means the lines are at right angles. Bisecting means cutting in half.)

For some questions, it helps to imagine that the point is connected to a line by a piece of string.

Rule: the point is always 1 cm from the line XY

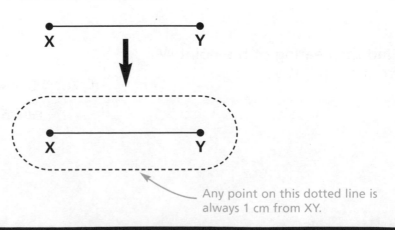

Any point on this dotted line is always 1 cm from XY.

QUESTIONS

1 Sketch the locus of a point that is always 2 cm from the outside of the triangle ABC.

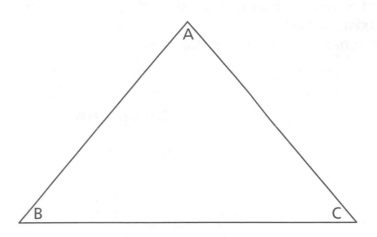

2 Look again at triangle ABC.
This time draw accurately the locus of a point that is always 2 cm from ABC.
We have started the question for you.

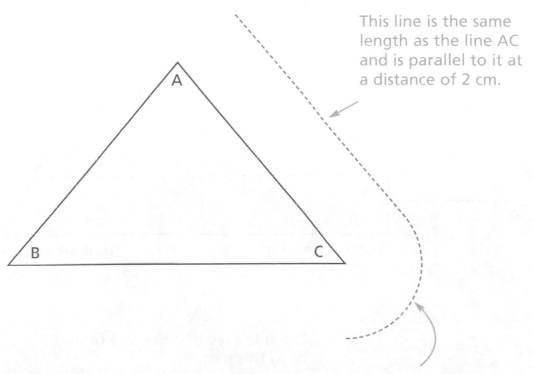

This line is the same length as the line AC and is parallel to it at a distance of 2 cm.

This curved line is exactly 2 cm from the point C. It was drawn using a pair of compasses.

WHAT YOU NEED TO KNOW

Look at this example:

A woman wants to plant a tree in her garden.
It must be at least 5 metres from the house and at least 3 metres from the trunk of an existing tree.
Shade the region where she can plant the tree.

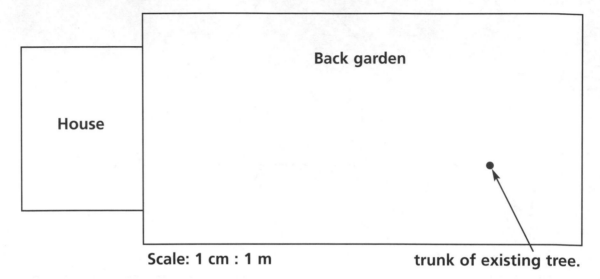

For this question we must use the scale provided.

Step 1: Draw a line 5 cm from the house on the plan.

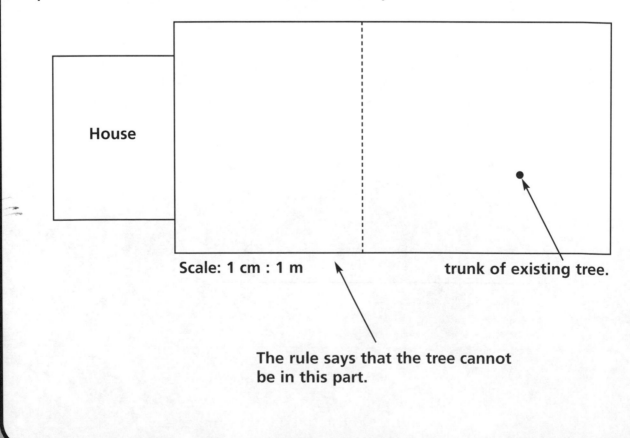

WHAT YOU NEED TO KNOW

Step 2: Use a pair of compasses to draw a line 3 cm from the tree trunk.

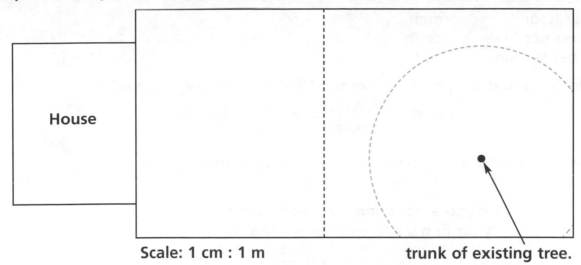

Scale: 1 cm : 1 m   trunk of existing tree.

Step 3: Shade in the region where the new tree can go.

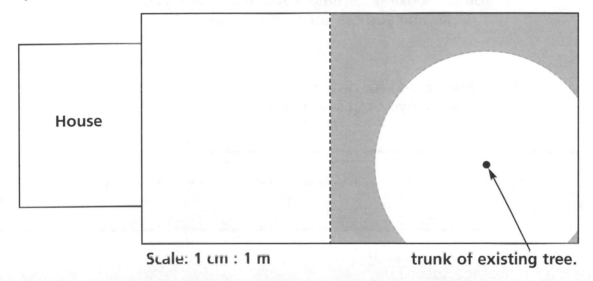

Scale: 1 cm : 1 m   trunk of existing tree.

QUESTION

1 A new skateboard ramp is to be built in the park. It has to be at least 50m from the Retirement Home and at least 20m from the centre of the ornamental pond. Shade the region where it could possibly be built.

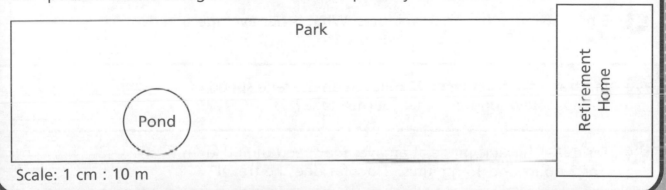

Scale: 1 cm : 10 m

WHAT YOU NEED TO KNOW

Speed is all about what distance can be travelled in a certain time:

miles per hour   mph
kilometres per hour   km/h
metres per second.   m/s

$$\text{speed} = \frac{\text{distance}}{\text{time}}$$

Example: Erica runs 9 miles in $1\frac{1}{2}$ hours. What is her average speed?

$$\text{speed} = \frac{\text{distance}}{\text{time}} = \frac{9}{1.5} = 6 \text{ mph}$$

It can be very helpful to represent speed, distance, time in a triangle:

If you are looking for speed, cover the S with your finger and you can see that D is above T.

$$S = \frac{D}{T}$$

If you are looking for time, cover the T with your finger and you can see that D is above S.

$$T = \frac{D}{S}$$

If you are looking for distance, cover the D with your finger and you can see that S is level with T.

$$D = S \times T$$

QUESTIONS

1 Albert drives 15 miles in half an hour.
What is his average speed?

----

2 Jasdeep runs around the 400m track in 93 seconds. What is her average speed? (Give your answer to one decimal place.)

----

3 Pete cycles 45 km in 2 hours. What is his average speed?

----

4 Emma swims 200 m in $3\frac{1}{2}$ minutes. What is her average speed?
(Don't forget to change the minutes to seconds.)

----

5 Jan travels a distance of 72 miles at an average speed of 36 mph. How long does her journey take?

----

6 Tariq flies his aeroplane at an average speed of 500 km/h for 2 hours and 15 minutes. How far does he travel?
